D1364083

THE MOST INFLUENTIAL
FEMALE
INVENTORS

BREAKING THE GLASS CEILING
THE MOST INFLUENTIAL WOMEN™

THE MOST INFLUENTIAL
FEMALE
INVENTORS

XINA M. UHL

Rosen
YA™
New York

To Brandy, Michaela, and Savannah, female inventors of the future

Published in 2019 by The Rosen Publishing Group, Inc.
29 East 21st Street, New York, NY 10010

Copyright © 2019 by The Rosen Publishing Group, Inc.

First Edition

All rights reserved. No part of this book may be reproduced in any form without permission in writing from the publisher, except by a reviewer.

Library of Congress Cataloging-in-Publication Data

Names: Uhl, Xina M., author.
Title: The most influential female inventors / Xina M. Uhl.
Description: New York : Rosen Publishing, 2019. | Series: Breaking the glass ceiling : the most influential women | Includes bibliographical references and index. | Audience: Grades 7–12.
Identifiers: LCCN 2017053229| ISBN 9781508179658 (library bound) | ISBN 9781508179801 (pbk.)
Subjects: LCSH: Women inventors—Juvenile literature.
Classification: LCC T36 .U39 2018 | DDC 609.2/52—dc23
LC record available at https://lccn.loc.gov/2017053229

Manufactured in the United States of America

On the cover: Marie Curie, pictured in her laboratory about 1906, became the first woman to win a Nobel Prize. Curie is the only woman to win in two different subject areas.

CONTENTS

An invention can be a machine, device, or system that has never been made or used before. It represents a different way to look at a problem and try to solve it, or it can make an existing process or action work better or do more. To invent something, a person must think "outside the box." She must have the ability to analyze what works and doesn't work, the creativity to think of different solutions, and the tenacity to tinker, fiddle, and attempt various methods of accomplishing her goals.

Entrepreneur magazine lists a number of traits common to inventors. They remain objective observers of their ideas and try not to get too attached to their original visions. They are demanding of themselves, as well as energetic, persistent, self-motivated, and inquisitive. They test their ideas and refine them. They embrace failure. As inventor Charles Lamprey said, they "fail fast and fail often."

Female inventors have done that in ways that influence our everyday lives today. For instance, Mary Anderson of Birmingham, Alabama, earned a patent in 1903 for a window-cleaning device—windshield wipers—after watching how much trouble a streetcar driver had seeing out of his windshield during a storm. Virginia Apgar created the Newborn

Dr. Virginia Apgar appears here in 1973. The Apgar score for newborn assessment is an acronym for Appearance, Pulse, Grimace, Activity, and Respiration. It was coined as a learning aid to help practicioners remember.

Scoring System, more commonly known as the Apgar Score, which is applied to newborn babies to assess their physical condition, a system that allows medical personnel to know what resources they need to dedicate to which children.

Annie Jump Cannon was one of the few women to work at Harvard University during the late 1800s. A scientist and astronomer, she developed a stellar classification system that was adopted worldwide and is still in use today. Throughout the centuries, female inventors have made valuable contributions in the areas of medicine and health, science, technology, the home, food and clothing, safety, business and commerce, and more.

Inventors are influenced by the world around them, by their cultures, families, nations, and their available resources. History records mostly male inventors for a variety of reasons. Females often lacked opportunities for education or were expected to remain within the home, cooking and caring for the children and the family, and discouraged from working outside the home in male-dominated industries. That does not mean that women did not invent things, however. It means that many women's contributions to invention and creation are lost in the annals of time.

Charlotte Smith lamented this fact in the 1891 newspaper called *The Woman Inventor*:

... [Women inventors] that have succeeded have done so only by their own self reliance and indomitable will power ... Deprived as woman is of her political power, and the obstacles thrown in her way; she has to face the contempt and scorn of her sex, while man looks on her as an intruder on his domain. All this has a tendency to hamper woman's inventive genius. How does the law recognize women? If she be married, her husband can take out the patent in his own name and sell her invention for his sole benefit give it away or refrain her from using it, and she has no remedy before the law.

Thankfully, opportunities for women have increased in the years since Smith wrote this. Today a better standard of living for everyday people—including greater opportunities in education and the workforce and changing attitudes toward women's potential— have allowed women to expand into roles that had previously been denied to them.

CHAPTER ONE

INVENTORS WHO HAVE NO NAMES: PREHISTORY

Archaeologists in Morocco in 2017 discovered skull fragments of early *Homo sapiens* dating to three hundred thousand years ago, proving that humans have been around longer than had previously been thought. But history does not start with the coming of human beings. Instead, it begins with the development of written records.

Because of the fact that writing did not exist until around 3000 BCE, many of the most fundamental inventions of the human species have gone unrecorded. Luckily, the funerary remains, pottery, tools, and weapons of ancient societies have been studied by archaeologists and anthropologists. Their findings have given us valuable information about the inventions made by early cultures prior to the development of writing.

The earliest people lived as nomads, traveling from place to place in search of food and pasture for their livestock. Men hunted game and women gathered plants and cared for young children. During this time period, there is no way to know which inventions were created by female inventors because the names of such people are lost. We can make educated guesses that women may have played key roles in medicine and healing by making use of plant life and in preparing food, as well as making clothing, ornamentation, art, and music.

The First Female Inventions

Likely inventions that were created by females, or that were refined by females, are some of the oldest human tools. The mortar and pestle is up to thirty thousand years old. It consists of a round stone that is either rolled or rubbed across a flat stone as a means of grinding grain. The grain is placed in a shallow depression in a stone surface called a mortar. The pestle, the round stone in the shape of a rod, is used to grind the grain into a finer state for consumption. Mortars and pestles have been used ever since, though not always for grains. They are also used to prepare pastes and spices, to grind down medical substances, and to assist chemists in making substances in the lab.

The remnants of these millstones appear in a bakery, or *pistrinum* in Latin, at Pompeii. Flour from them would have been baked in the oven, the structure beside the millstones.

Similar to the mortar and pestle, but more mechanical in nature, is the millstone, thought to be developed around 5000 BCE. The principle is the same as with the mortar and pestle—grinding grain between two stones. However, millstones are considerably larger than the mortar and pestle and were turned by animal power. Good examples of millstones occur in the Roman town of Pompeii. Pompeii was buried in ash from the eruption of Mount Vesuvius in 79 CE, which preserved the city for later discovery. The large millstones consist of a stone pedestal with a conelike top. Set over the top of it is a large hollowed stone that is designed to have an opening on the side where a wooden beam was inserted. The beam would have been attached to the harness of a mule or donkey and the animal would walk in a circle around the millstone, turning it. Grain was poured into the top of the funneled stone and rotated around the lower stone, which was fixed into the ground. Then the flour was collected at the base.

Related to the grinding of flour is the creation of the oven at about 9000 BCE. It allowed for a permanent

The opium poppy was first cultivated in Southwest Asia around 3400 BCE. The Sumerians called it the joy plant.

structure that contained heat, unlike fires in the open air. Once early peoples began to cultivate crops, or create agriculture, people began to gather in villages and cities. The cultivation of wheat and barley is dated to about 7500 BCE. The cultivation of olives, so important in the ancient Mediterranean, came

THE EARLIEST WOMAN?

In 1974, a scientist named Donald Johanson was driving a Land Rover through a gully in Ethiopia. He and a companion named Tom Gray were looking for fossils when they stumbled upon a very special bone. It was a forearm. Next, they located a skull bone, then other fragments: a femur, some ribs, a piece of a lower jaw, and a pelvis. Over a period of a few weeks, they recovered about 40 percent of a single skeleton.

During the celebration at their camp, the Beatles' song "Lucy in the Sky with Diamonds" was playing, and the scientists decided they would name their skeleton Lucy. For many years, she was thought to be the oldest hominid (a human ancestor) in the world, at 3.18 million years old. Lucy did not look much like human women, though. She would have weighed between sixty and sixty-five pounds (twenty-seven to twenty-nine kilograms) and stood around 3.5 feet (1 m) tall. She was probably covered with hair and had an ape-shaped head with a jutting jaw.

later at about 3500 BCE. The opium poppy was cultivated at about the same time. Opium is extracted from the poppy's seedpod and provides a potent drug to relieve pain. Leavened bread dates from about 2600 BCE. Leavening causes bread to rise, creating a lighter food.

Vessels

The invention of pottery came around 13,000 BCE. These containers were made of clay and hardened with fire. The simplest way of making pottery is to form long ropes of clay and place them one on top of another in a bowl shape. The ropes of clay are smoothed over, and the vessel is hardened in flames. The earliest form of pottery is earthenware. It allows water to seep through unless it is covered in a glaze, a substance melted under high heat.

The decoration of pottery through painting is found beginning in 6500 BCE. Archeologists have been able to identify and track whole civilizations by studying the designs on pottery and dating them. The potter's wheel came along in 3500 BCE. This is a round, flat surface upon which a lump of clay is placed. The surface—a wheel—spins around, allowing the potter to shape the item and keep the sides even. The kiln was invented at about the same time. This is an oven capable of reaching high temperatures, and it is used to produce more durable pottery.

The Arts

Cave paintings and the paintbrushes invented to create them also date far back into human history, between 30,000 and 40,000 BCE. Many caves in Europe contain prehistoric artwork of horses, bison, and people engaged in hunts. The art may have

Cave paintings in the Lascaux Cave of southwestern France display magnificent likenesses of animals and humans. The Lascaux Cave has been closed to visitors since 1963 to preserve it.

sacred meaning, perhaps to call on divine beings to assist hunters in finding prey animals. Cave art has also been discovered in other parts of the world, including Asia, Africa, Australia, and North and South America.

At around 6000 BCE, the drum came into existence. By 3000 BCE, the harp and lyre also created music for enjoyment and sacred ceremonies. Basket weaving dates to 5500 BCE. Just like pottery, baskets were often woven with intricate styles, and their designs can be used to date different communities.

Cloth

Leather began to be tanned around 5000 BCE, and the loom dates to about the same time. The loom is a device used to weave cloth. The device is made of bars or beams in a frame, with two sets of parallel threads alternating with one another. When one set of threads is raised, it forms the warp. A cross thread is called a weft, and it is carried through the warp by a block of wood called a shuttle.

At about 2600 BCE, legend says that a fourteen-year-old Chinese girl named Xilingshi, the wife of the emperor Huang Di, invented a loom to weave silk. The secret of how to make silk—which originates from the silkworm— was kept by the Chinese for three thousand years until silkworms were taken to Japan along with four Chinese girls who taught the Japanese how to work with silk. Another legend says that a Chinese princess married a prince from India. As she traveled to her new home, she carried the eggs of silkworm and mulberry seeds in her headdress. That is how silk is said to have come to India.

CHAPTER TWO

THE LONG MARCH OF TIME: ANTIQUITY TO THE EIGHTEENTH CENTURY

C ivilizations became more complex as the years passed. Societies in Egypt, Mesopotamia, and Crete left lasting monuments in stone and in writings, such as stories, songs, and poems. Still, though, inventors were seldom named. But as before, many women may have been involved in the creation of inventions, such as the corset in 1900 BCE. The corset is a piece of women's clothing that is designed to constrict the waist and emphasize the bosom. The art of the Minoans who lived on Crete show women wearing corsets. Gloves and shoes came into being by 1500 BCE. Knitting debuted at 1000 BCE. It involves creating fabric by using strings of yarn to interlock using knitting needles, or specially shaped wooden sticks. A Greek poet by the name of Hesiod spoke of *piloi* in the eighth century BCE. These early socks were made from matted animal hairs and placed in shoes to line them.

Other items generally associated with women are soap and shampoo, which date from about 150 CE, tapestries (600 CE), the folding fan (650 CE), and the kimono, which dates to 700 CE.

The Divine Maria

Maria the Jewess is known to history by several names, including Maria Hebraea, Maria the Hebrew, and the Divine Maria. She lived in Egypt in the first or second century BCE, and by all accounts she was an influential and memorable woman, though little is known about her as a person; instead, her work lives on through the writings of Zosimus the Panopolitan. He was the first Greek author to write about alchemy, or the science whose goal was to turn metal into gold. Alchemy used many chemical processes in its vain quest to achieve the impossible, but it did further human knowledge about chemistry.

Maria the Jewess invented and constructed various ovens and cooking utensils in order to distill metal, clay, and glass. She used caulk made of fat, wax, starch paste, fatty clay, and the "clay of the philosophers." She preferred to use glass vessels for their transparency and ability to safely manipulate mercury, "the deadly poison, since it dissolves gold, and the most injurious of metals." Another deadly poison, arsenic, she used to prepare "divine water."

This image of Maria the Jewess, also known as Maria Hebræa or Maria the Hebrew, was published in the 1702 edition of *Bibliotheca Chemica Curiosa*, or the *Library of Chemical Curiosities*.

The vessel she is most famous for is the bain-marie, or double boiler. This device contains an outer pot filled with water, while the inner pot contains a chemical substance, which is heated moderately. Maria the Jewess may or may not have been the first person to use it, but its creation has been attributed to her and derives its name, from the French, from her name.

Maria the Jewess also gave the oldest description of the still, which consists of three parts: the vessel containing the substance to be heated and distilled, a cooler part to condense the vapor, and a receiver, which holds the distillation. The Greek name of the still was *kerotakis*. It was used to soften metals and mix them with different coloring agents in order to attempt to change base metals into gold or silver.

She appears to have believed, like other Alexandrian alchemists, that every substance or material found in nature was basically one. She is said to have cried out, "one becomes two, two becomes three, and by means of the third and fourth achieves unity; thus two are but one." Later alchemists quoted this with certain variations. She also believed that the human body was made of liquids, solids, and the spirit. Her writings and work influenced later scholars, such as Arabian alchemist Al-Habib and tenth-century author Abu Abdullah Muhammad ibn Umail al-Tamimi, who called her Maria the Sage.

A Chinese Hero

Sometime around 1240 CE, a girl was born in China. Her name is lost to history. She became known as Granny Huang. As a young girl, she was forced to work for her adopted parents in poor conditions. She escaped by climbing out of the thatched roof of her parents' home and ran away to the town of Yazhou, or modern-day Sanya. There, she lived for thirty-some years before returning to her hometown of Songjiang. With her, she brought knowledge of a new way of processing cotton. Until then, in order to weave with cotton, the seeds had to be cleaned out of raw cotton by hand. The fibers would then be beaten and finally spun using a hand-powered spinning wheel, which allowed for only one spindle to be turned at a time.

Granny Huang developed a cotton gin with two rollers that could clean cottonseeds far faster than could be accomplished by hand. She also showed the people how to improve the process of untangling and fluffing up the cotton. She did this by using wooden clappers tied to a wooden bow. Finally, she built a spinning wheel with three spindles that was operated by a treadle. It allowed one person to spin multiple threads at one time. These innovations allowed the town of Songjiang, in what was once a desperately poor region, to become one of the richest in China. Raw cotton was grown elsewhere and shipped to Songjiang so that it could be made into handkerchiefs, belts, mattresses, and beautiful jacquard quilts. Granny Huang was honored as a national hero.

THE TERRIBLE SCOURGE

Smallpox is an infectious disease that causes a high fever, headache, back pain, and pockmarks known as pox that cover the face and body. One of the world's most devastating diseases, it killed up to 30 percent of its victims—mainly children—and left survivors with sometimes disfiguring scars. The disease may date back to the third century BCE in Egypt, although this is a controversial claim. From China in the fourth century CE comes the earliest written description of a disease that is probably smallpox. The spread of the disease throughout the world followed in the wake of global expansion, exploration, and trade routes.

Modern vaccination came into being with the 1796 experiments of English doctor Edward Jenner, who exposed several people to cowpox and then tested whether they would later be immune to smallpox. They were.

Vaccination spread over the following years, and in 1959 the World Health Organization (WHO) launched a campaign to rid the world of smallpox. On May 8, 1980, the WHO officially declared that the disease had been eradicated, one of the greatest achievements in public health.

The Western world did not know of these improvements to weaving until centuries later, when the spinning jenny was invented, and afterward came Eli Whitney's cotton gin, patented in 1794.

Cowpox and Smallpox

Hundreds of years passed before the name of another woman inventor comes to the fore. This is Lady Mary Wortley Montagu (1689–1762), the wife of the English ambassador to Istanbul from 1716 to 1718. As a young woman, she contracted smallpox, which left her scarred. In Europe at the time there was no treatment for smallpox beyond ineffective procedures such as bloodletting, enemas, and inducing vomiting. However, in Turkey inoculation to diseases such as cowpox (a form of smallpox suffered by cattle) was known. Fluid would be taken from the lesions of cattle that suffered from cowpox and administered to children, who would not develop smallpox. Intrigued by this practice, Montagu had her son successfully inoculated by the embassy surgeon.

Afterward, she undertook a campaign of letter writing in an effort to bring this discovery to England. However, her ideas encountered strong opposition by church authorities and some physicians. Montagu saw to it that family members were inoculated, and whenever possible she spread the news about this means of stopping the spread of smallpox. Royalty and well-to-do people in Europe and America adopted

Lady Mary Wortley Montagu, shown here in Turkish-style attire, is most famous for her letters. She is also known as a colorful feminist and traveler.

this practice, but it was cumbersome and difficult, so it did not spread beyond the rich and selected military units.

In 1724, Dr. Emmanuel Timoni, who had been the Montagus' family physician in Istanbul, submitted a scientific description of vaccination to the Royal Society, which included firsthand accounts from the ambassador to Tripoli of the success of inoculation in Tripoli, Tunis, and Algiers, as well as other Muslim territories. Inoculation was adopted in England and France about fifty years before the discovery was advanced and refined by Edward Jenner.

Corn, Thread, and Comets

The 1700s and early 1800s saw an expansion in industry and science in Europe. The first female American inventor was Sybilla Masters, who in 1712 devised a new method for cleaning and curing corn. Because there was no patent office in America at this time, she traveled to London to file for one. The patent was granted in her husband's name, however, because she was a woman. The economy of Pennsylvania prospered because of Masters's invention. Later, she filed for another patent for a material that used palmetto leaves in bonnets, another successful endeavor.

By 1793, when the next American woman inventor came along, the country had established its own patent office. Hannah Slater came up with an improved cotton sewing thread.

Joseph Brown, sc

Caroline Herschel.

ÆTAT 92

At the age of seventy-seven, Caroline Herschel received a gold medal from the Astronomical Society for her impressive volume of work.

Caroline Herschel (1750–1848) was a German singer who served as an apprentice to her brother, a British astronomer. She assisted her brother by keeping house and grinding and polishing mirrors. She developed the modern mathematical approach to astronomy when she completed the calculations that went along with her brother's observations. Along the way, she discovered comets and nebulae and became the first person to be paid by the British government for her scientific contributions. The catalog in which she listed every discovery she and her brother made is still in use.

CHAPTER THREE

NEW DAYS DAWN: EARLY NINETEENTH CENTURY WOMEN

Until the late 1700s, the creation of products was usually done in people's homes, using hand tools or very basic machines. Most people lived on farms, raising their own animals and crops. In Great Britain after 1750, food production had increased, freeing up money for families to purchase goods that had been manufactured. Booming trade and cotton markets strengthened banks. The age of science and invention had dawned, and three important changes occurred. First, machines were invented to do work that had always been done with hand tools. Second, steam power took the place of power generated by animals and humans. Finally, the factory system came into being, increasing productivity to a staggering degree.

People began to move from rural communities to the big cities to find work in factories. Transportation changed with the development of

WOMEN IN THE INDUSTRIAL REVOLUTION

When people left their farming lives in the country to take up wage work in large cities, life for women changed drastically. In poor families, children also worked in factories. Women worked in factories as well, often on menial tasks. They earned less than half of men's wages, and according to the law their salaries went to their husbands, or if they were unmarried, to their fathers. Hours were long, usually fourteen to sixteen hours a day, six days a week. Women's health suffered. For instance, women who performed the detailed stitching required of lace makers had to wear wooden rods for support; otherwise their slouching over created rounded and deformed chests. In the textile mills, the dusty air gave women lung disease.

Because of the long hours and difficult working conditions, women often quit when they married and began to raise a family. While women had always worked prior to the Industrial Revolution, there now existed a divide between work performed at home and that performed for pay. This divide persists still.

steamships, railroads, and streetcars. The first wave of what became known as the Industrial Revolution saw the movement of textile manufacturing from homes to factories. The invention of the cotton gin and steam power dominated in the period from the late 1700s through the mid-1800s. In the mid-

1800s, the second wave of the Industrial Revolution took place, lasting through the early 1900s. Companies and factories grew in size and made use of technology to produce goods in mass quantities. The invention of electricity and a new process for making steel dominated.

Life changed for most people. Cities became crowded, dirty, and unsanitary. Working conditions were poor, with long hours, child labor, and dangerous machinery. Automobiles debuted, and slowly replaced the horse and buggy and railroads as the dominant form of transportation.

All this change caused both prosperity and difficulties. It also provided opportunities for women inventors.

Solving Problems: Mechanical and Social

Sarah Guppy Coote (1770–1852) leaves behind an impressive legacy as a designer, engineer, inventor, author, reformer, and mother of six. After marrying the wealthy Samuel Guppy, she moved to Bristol, England, where she spent her adult life.

Her first patent came in 1811 for "erecting and constructing bridges and rail-roads without arches or sterlings, whereby the danger of being washed away by floods is available." She advocated for a suspension bridge in Clifton and served as an early investor for the project. When Thomas Telford

The Menai Suspension Bridge was the first major suspension bridge in the world. It bridged the Menai Strait and joined the island of Anglesey with mainland Wales.

asked for permission to use her patented invention she gave it to him free of charge. This gained her acknowledgment in the bridge design used in the Menai Bridge.

She also patented a bed that reclined and served as an exercise machine, a means of caulking wooden ships, and a tea and coffee pot attachment that used steam to poach eggs and warm toast. She created a means of recycling manure from the roadsides to use as fertilizer, identified safety improvements for railways, and tried to treat foot rot in sheep with a tobacco solution. She also left behind numerous designs for improvements to candlesticks, stones, and other appliances. Her humanitarian efforts involved founding the Society for the Reward and Encouragement of Virtuous, Faithful, and Industrious Female Servants, work on housing widows and spinsters, and funded living spaces for indigent sailors. At the age of sixty-six, after the death of her first husband, she married Charles Eyre Coote, who was just thirty-three years old. He burned through her fortune quickly. She registered her final patent—for caulking ship hulls—at the age of seventy-three.

The World's First Computer Programmer

Ada Lovelace (1815–1852) was a mathematician and the daughter of the poet Lord Byron. She introduced many computer concepts by translating

Countess Ada Lovelace was the daughter of the poet Lord Byron. Like her famous father, she died young, at only thirty-six years of age.

and annotating an article on invention written by Charles Babbage—her notes made the article three times longer than the original piece. In her annotations, published in 1843, she described how codes could be created for an analytical engine. This procedure would handle letters and symbols along with numbers, and it predicted the possibilities of Babbage's machine. In essence, Lovelace came up with a method that would allow the engine to repeat a series of instructions. This process is known as looping and is used in modern computer programs. For this invention, she is considered the first computer programmer—without even having a computer to work on.

Another notable mathematician was Russian Sonja Kovalevsky (1850–1891), who developed Kovalevsky's theorem, which dealt with partial differential equations. She also served as the editor of *Acta Mathematica*.

Kovalevsky showed a talent for mathematics at an early age but faced barriers because of her gender. Women were not allowed to study in Russian universities, and her father objected to her studying abroad—calling it "improper." She went to Germany despite this and studied with Karl Weierstrass. For her 1888 work, "On the Problem of the Rotation of a Solid Body about a Fixed Point," she was awarded the famous Prix Bordin of the French Academy of Sciences.

War and More

Englishwoman Henrietta Vansittart (1833–1883) was the daughter of James Lowe, the inventor of screw propellers for steamships. After her father's death, Vansittart improved his work by inventing a propeller that was used on the famous ocean liner the *Lusitania*, which was torpedoed by a German submarine during World War I. She gave recognition to her father by naming it the Lowe-Vansittart Propeller. As a woman in the male-dominated discipline of engineering, she so impressed her colleagues that her obituary called her "a remarkable personage with a great knowledge of engineering matters and considerable versatility of talent."

Her personal life was more controversial, though. She married rich and had an affair with Edward Bulwer Lytton, a cabinet secretary. However, a combination of mania and anthrax sent her to a lunatic asylum to live out her last days.

When she became a widow at the age of twenty-one, Martha Hunt Coston (1826–1904) provided for her four children by developing a maritime signal flare system used during the American Civil War. Coston built upon the signal flare system originally conceived by her deceased husband. His system had not worked, but Coston spent a long period of time perfecting her husband's idea. She wrote about how "the men I employed and dismissed, the

The sinking of the British passenger ship the *Lusitania* killed about 1,200 of the around 1,950 people aboard it and contributed to the US decision to enter World War I.

experiments I made myself, the frauds that were practiced upon me, almost disheartened me."

However, she managed to head up a team of chemists, which used fireworks technology to create

"pyrotechnic night signals." The US Navy used these signals in order to save the lives of shipwreck victims. Later improvements to her system allowed her to market her signals to yacht clubs, navies, and merchant shippers worldwide. As a woman in a "man's world," she described having to "fight like a lioness" for proper notice and compensation.

CHAPTER FOUR

INDUSTRY RAMPS UP: LATE NINETEENTH CENTURY WOMEN

I n 1869, Harriet Morrison Irwin (1828–1897) made American architectural history. She became the first woman to patent a design for a hexagonal, or six-sided, house. Her design had no hallways or four-cornered rooms and made more efficient use of space than a rectangular building as well as having better airflow. As she noted in her patent application, "The objects of my invention are the economizing of space and building-materials, the obtaining of economical heating mediums, thorough lighting and ventilation, and facilities for inexpensive ornamentation."

Irwin's motivation in creating such a house came from a lifelong affliction with respiratory and intestinal problems. She wanted to design a practical, economical home for invalid housekeepers. She had no formal training in architecture, being instead self-taught. After obtaining her patent, her husband, James Patton Irwin, and her brother-in-law formed a land company called Hill and Irwin, in order to promote her hexagonal home design. While two homes were said to have been inspired by this design in the Charlotte, North Carolina, area where she lived, both of them have since been demolished.

Irwin went on to give birth to nine children, of whom five survived infancy. She published a novel in 1871—*The Hermit of Petraea*—in order to promote her patent. The protagonist in the novel found increased health and well-being in a hexagonal home in Arabia.

A Lifelong Inventor

Prior to 1870, a trip to the grocery store was missing one crucial element: a paper bag to contain customers' purchases. Instead, shoppers would have to take their purchases home in a rolled-up cone of paper or using envelopelike bags that could not stand upright. Enter inventor Margaret E. Knight (1838–1914), who showed a knack for invention while still a young child. She didn't play with dolls, but instead, as she said, "the only things I wanted were a jack-knife, a gimlet, and pieces of wood. My friends were horrified. I was called a tomboy ... I was always making things for my brothers ... I was famous for my kites; and my sleds were the envy and admiration of all the boys in town."

One day, twelve-year-old Margaret visited her older brothers at the Manchester, New Hampshire, cotton mill where they worked. As she watched, a loom shuttle broke free from its spool of thread and stabbed a young worker. She devised a device that kept the shuttles from breaking free of the loom, thereby improving worker safety. Soon, mills all across New England implemented her design. Because she did not have a patent on the design, she did not profit from the invention.

Years later, Knight got a job at the Columbia Paper Bag Company in Springfield, Massachusetts. There she worked ten-hour days making flat-bottomed paper bags by hand, for somewhere between $1.50 and $3.50 a week. The bags had to be made by hand in an expensive, labor-intensive process. Knight decided to improve the process and after two years of effort, she came up with a flat-bottomed paper-bag machine that did the work of thirty people. After a lawsuit in which a man tried to steal the machine's design and claim it as his own, Knight received a patent for her invention in 1871. The use of her machine spread worldwide, earning her a Royal Legion of Honor from Queen Victoria.

Knight then went on to receive patents for a number of different devices, including a machine designed to cut out shoe soles, a clasp for robes, a sewing machine reel, an "automatic tool for boring concave or cylindrical surfaces," a dress

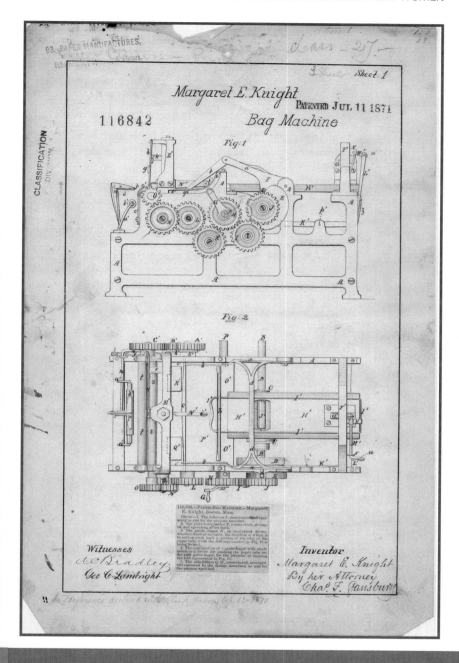

This drawing of Margaret E. Knight's paper bag machine was submitted along with her patent application. She finally received her patent in 1871.

and skirt protector, and a sleeve-valve engine. She received six patents alone for shoe manufacturing. Over her lifetime, she received twenty-seven patents. When she died, her portrait was hung in the Patent Office in Washington D.C. Obituaries called her a "woman Edison."

SEXISM AND RACISM IN THE LATE 1800S

The author, editor, and publisher of the 1890 broadsheet "The Woman Inventor" was Charlotte Smith, an enthusiastic advocate for feminism. Though not an inventor herself, Smith became intrigued with the accomplishments of women inventors in the late nineteenth century. She pressured the Inventors and Manufacturers Association in the United States to admit women as members and campaigned over a ten-year period for the US Patent Office to compile and publish a list of patents granted to women. Her efforts led to two publications, which covered the time period from 1790 to 1892 and listed some four thousand women inventors. She also founded and presided over the Women Inventors' Mutual Aid and Protective Association in 1891.

In "The Woman Inventor," Smith told the story of a black inventor by the name of Ellen F. Eglin. Born in 1849, Eglin worked as a housekeeper in Washington, D.C., when she invented a more efficient clothes wringer for washing machines. In 1888, she sold her invention for only $18 to a white agent, who took it and made a considerable amount of money off it.

When Smith asked her why she had worked so hard at her invention only to sell it so cheaply, Eglin replied, "You know I am black, and if it was known that a Negro woman patented the invention, white ladies would not buy the wringer."

Undaunted, Eglin began to work on another device, with plans to showcase it at the Woman's International Industrial Inventors Congress. There, she said, "Women are invited to participate regardless of color lines." It is unknown what this invention might have been, nor how and when she died.

A Ghost in the Kitchen?

Amanda Theodosia Jones (1835–1914) was born in East Bloomfield, New York, one of thirteen children. At just fifteen, she began a teaching career at a local school. A bout of tuberculosis in her youth caused her to struggle with ill health her entire life. During the 1850s, she became an adherent of spiritualism, which encouraged contact with the dead through the use of a medium. Jones considered herself a medium, and in 1869 she moved to Chicago as a result of advice she said she had received from spirits. She believed that the ghost of her deceased brother visited her and told her that the preservation

This color poster for the World's Columbian Exposition of 1893, also known as the Chicago World's Fair, acknowledged the anniversary of the Chicago Fire.

of fruit could be done in a better way. With this message as inspiration, she experimented until she came up with the Jones Process, a device that vacuum-packed fresh fruit. She received a patent for this invention in 1872. In 1905 and 1906, she received patents for the use of dehydration to sterilize and preserve food.

In 1880, she was granted a patent for improving how oil was delivered to a burner for generating steam, smelting metal, manufacturing glass, and similar applications. In 1904, 1912, and 1914, she received three more patents for further refinements to oil burners. All in all, she obtained twelve patents.

In addition to her inventions, she published several books of poems and an autobiography before dying of influenza in 1914.

Although Josephine G. Cochran's 1886 invention was not inspired by a ghostly visitation, it did involve food. As a well-to-do woman who liked to entertain at her home, she hoped to find a machine that could wash dishes more quickly than a person could and without breaking any. Unable to find such a thing, she invented it herself. First, she created wire compartments, then placed them inside of a wheel, which lay inside a copper boiler. This invention—the first practical dishwasher— was shown at the 1893 Chicago World's Fair. The company Cochran founded to manufacture the dishwashers is now known as KitchenAid.

These babies wear cloth diapers like those invented by Maria E. Allen. Cloth diapers are often considered more environmentally responsible than disposable diapers because they are not placed in landfills.

For the Children

Other inventions of note from the late 1800s include the cloth diaper, patented in 1887 by Maria E. Allen. Her diaper consisted "of a layer of cotton wadding, above a sheet of paper, the latter being covered by a fine gauze material." The diaper was held in place by pins and was designed so that the inner lining could be disposed of while the outer diaper remained clean.

Anna Connelly of Philadelphia, Pennsylvania, was granted a patent in 1887 for a fire escape. It was designed as a bridge with an iron railing that was placed between the roofs of adjacent buildings to allow inhabitants to escape from one roof to another.

In 1889, Anna Breadin received a patent for the school desk. Made from wood, it had curved metal legs and could be folded and stored under a table. Many schoolhouses used these strong, durable desks into the twentieth century.

CHAPTER FIVE

WOMEN GAIN GROUND: EARLY TWENTIETH CENTURY

I n 1902, a Birmingham, Alabama, woman by the name of Mary Anderson (1866–1953) visited New York City. As she rode a streetcar on a freezing, wet day, she noticed that the driver could hardly see through the sleet covering the windshield. Several times, he had to get out of the vehicle to clean it off. She realized that the driver would benefit from a blade that wiped the moisture off the windshield.

Though she had to design several models, Anderson eventually came up with a prototype of windshield wiper arms made of rubber and wood, which were attached to the inside of the vehicle via a lever. In 1903, she was awarded a patent for her window-cleaning device. Her efforts to sell the

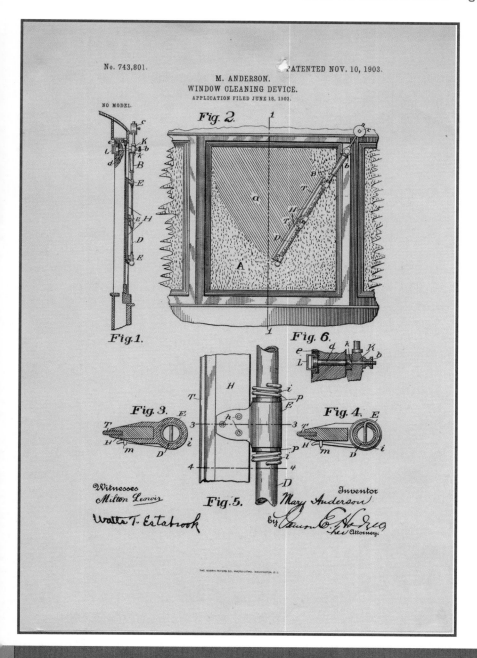

Mary Anderson's window cleaning device is shown here in this patent diagram. Her windshield wipers never became a commercial success.

idea to a Canadian manufacturer failed, and critics complained that such an apparatus would distract drivers. Though she never earned money from her invention, she was inducted into the Inventors Hall of Fame in 2011.

African American Women Make Waves

In 1867, Sarah Breedlove was born on a plantation in Delta, Louisiana. By seven years old, she was working in the cotton fields, and by fourteen she married. She became a widow when she was twenty. She moved to St. Louis and got work as a laundress and cook. By the time she was thirty-five, she had married again, but she worried about her future. She told the *New York Times*, "As I bent over the washboard and looked at my arms buried in soapsuds, I said to myself: 'What are you going to do when you grow old and your back gets stiff? Who is going to take care of your little girl?'"

In the 1890s, her hair began to fall out as a result of a scalp ailment, causing her to devise home remedies and experiment with store-bought treatments. Her 1905 formula for creating smooth, shiny, straightened hair was known as the Walker Method or the Walker System. She got married again, after leaving her second husband—to Charles J. Walker—and changed her name to Madame C. J. Walker. With the encouragement and help of her

Madam C. J. Walker is shown here around 1914. In addition to selling her beauty products, she also invested shrewdly in real estate in Harlem, New York.

husband, they created advertisements for African American hair treatments. She employed door-to-door saleswomen to market her products to women in the black community. In doing so, she became one of the first American businesswomen to become a millionaire.

She moved to Harlem, New York, operated her business, and donated money to scholarships, old-age homes, the National Association for the Advancement of Colored People, and the National Conference on Lynching. Walker died at the age of fifty-one from hypertension.

Marjorie Steward Joyner is shown here in the late 1960s. She was one of the first African American women to receive a patent.

Marjorie Stewart Joyner (1896–1994) worked as a vice president of the Madam C. J. Walker Company, where she trained thousands of African American beauticians. She invented the permanent wave machine and received a patent for it in 1928 and another patent in 1929 for a scalp protector to make these "perms" more comfortable.

THE BUSINESS OF BEAUTY

Women inventors often develop products that benefit women, such as cosmetics, but few become powerhouses of business like Elizabeth Arden (1884–1966). Born Florence Nightingale Graham in Woodbridge, Ontario, in Canada, Arden moved to New York City at thirty years old. She worked with a chemist to develop a beauty cream, a new product at the time. She opened a salon on Fifth Avenue in 1910. A trip to Paris in 1912 inspired her to bring eye makeup to American women, and by 1915 her products were sold internationally. At the time of her death at age eighty-one, more than one hundred of her salons were located across the world. Arden's company reported more than $1 billion in sales as of June 2007.

Fashion designer Coco Chanel (1883–1971) was born in Saumur, France, where she grew up in an orphanage. In 1910, she opened up a shop selling

(continued on the next page)

(continued from the previous page)

hats, and in the 1920s she created perfumes. In 1921, Chanel No. 5 became the first perfume sold globally; it remains in production to this day. Over time, she introduced a number of suits, along with a "little black dress." Fashion designer Christian Dior described her contribution when he said, "With a black pullover and 10 rows of pearls, she revolutionized fashion." *Forbes* reports that as of 2017, the Chanel company was worth more than $7 billion.

Ma Rainey (1886–1939), born Gertrude Bridgett, is known as the Mother of the Blues for her reinvention of music in the 1910s and 1920s. At fourteen years of age, she made her musical debut in a talent show, and after marrying a vaudeville performer by the name of Pa Rainey, the couple toured as a song and dance act. She first heard the music that would later become known as the blues in 1902 while in a small town in Missouri. Incorporating the music into her jazz and jug-band performances, she became famous for her deep, strong voice.

Beginning in 1923, she recorded music for the Paramount company, eventually recording ninety-two songs with titles like "Oh Papa Blues" and "Trust No Man." She became wildly popular and left her stamp on a uniquely American music form.

Ma Rainey is shown here with other members of the Ma Rainey Georgia Jazz Band around 1924 or 1925. Her singular style reinvented the music of her time.

An Atomic Woman

A French scientist born in Poland, Marie Curie (1867–1934) was part of a team that worked with radioactive substances and gave birth to the field of atomic physics. She won the Nobel Prize for Physics twice. In 1903, she shared the prize with her husband, Pierre Curie, and fellow scientist Henri Becquerel, becoming the first woman to be so honored. In 1911, she again won a Nobel Prize, this time by herself, and in chemistry, becoming the only person to have won Nobel Prizes in two different fields.

Maria Salomea Sklodowska was born in Warsaw, Poland. Because women could not study at a university in Poland, she moved to Paris, France, where she earned degrees in physics and math in only three years. She and French scientist Pierre Curie, with whom she worked, married in 1895. When Henri Becquerel found out that the element uranium gave off energy rays, Marie began studying the energy, which she called radioactivity. Within two years, the Curies had discovered two elements: radium and polonium, which led to their award of the 1903 Nobel Prize.

In 1906, Pierre Curie was killed when he was struck by a horse-drawn wagon on a Paris street. She assumed his teaching position at Sorbonne University to become the first female professor there. She won a second Nobel Prize, in chemistry this time, in 1911 for isolating pure radium.

During World War I, she and one of her two daughters (Irene, who was only seventeen years old) established medical units near battle lines in order to enable wounded soldiers to obtain X-rays. More than one million soldiers benefited from these radiology units.

After the war, Curie devoted her energy to using radioactive substances in medicine. In 1934, she died of leukemia from exposure to radioactivity. Her lab books were radioactive many years after her death. Curie's discoveries led to countless benefits in science, industry, and medicine.

The death of Marie Curie's husband, Pierre, in a traffic accident, caused her to devote her considerable energy to completing the work that she and her husband had done together.

Medicine and More

Louise Pearce (1885–1959) was the first female research pathologist at the Rockefeller Institute in 1920. Pearce, two chemists, and fellow pathologist Wade Hampton Brown, developed an arsenic-based treatment for trypanosomiasis, also known as African sleeping sickness. The compound the team developed, tryparsamide, cured the illness in animals. However, the team needed human subjects to test it on. When an outbreak of the disease occurred in the Belgium Congo, Pearce volunteered to go. The Rockefeller Institute sent her, "trusting her vigorous personality to carry out an assignment none too easy for a woman physician and not without its dangers." She administered the treatment to more than seventy patients, which succeeded in curing them within a few weeks. For her service, Pearce received the order of the Crown of Belgium, and in 1953, the Royal Order of the Lion.

Pearce also studied syphilis in rabbits, for which tryparsamide was standard treatment until penicillin replaced it. With Brown, she discovered the Brown-Pearce tumor, the first known tumor capable of being transplanted. This tumor helped to further cancer research in laboratory settings.

Pearce was thought to be a lesbian, and she shared a New Jersey home with two women before her death in 1959.

Other notable inventions developed by women in the early twentieth century included an early version of Monopoly called the Landlord's Game, by Elizabeth Phillips in 1904; the bra, created by Mary P. Jacobs in 1914; the electric hot water heater, developed by Ida Forbes in 1924; and in 1927 Anna Wagner Keichline invented K Brick, a substance which led to the development of today's concrete block.

Lillian Moller Gilbreth (1878–1972) invented a number of well-known kitchen innovations, including the egg keeper, butter tray, and other door shelves in refrigerators, and the trash can operated by a foot pedal. She patented an improved electric can opener and a washing machine wastewater hose. Her other accomplishments included becoming Purdue University's first female engineering professor and raising twelve children. The mother in the movie *Cheaper by the Dozen* was modeled after her.

CHAPTER SIX

WOMEN, WAR, AND MORE: MID-TWENTIETH CENTURY

From the time she left her native Austria and landed in Hollywood, Hedy Lamarr (1914–2000) made a splash on the silver screen. Born Hedwig Eva Maria (Hedy) Kiesler in Vienna, she was proficient in piano and dance and spoke four languages by the time she was ten years old. At sixteen, she starred in a German film and at eighteen she appeared nude in a Czech film called *Ecstasy*. She married an arms manufacturer named Fritz Mandl in 1933. In Lamarr's autobiography, she reported that Mandl dealt with the Italian dictator Benito Mussolini and had Adolf Hitler as a guest in their home. She soon fled the marriage and made her way to the United States.

Actress, model, and inventor Hedy Lamarr once said, "Any girl can be glamorous. All you have to do is stand still and look stupid."

A glamorous, raven-haired beauty, she acted for movie studio Metro-Goldwyn-Mayer from 1938 to 1945. Once dubbed the "world's most beautiful woman," she grew unsatisfied with the mostly decorative parts she played. She set up her own production company in 1946 and went on to star in her most famous role yet, a Cecil B. DeMille epic called *Samson and Delilah*.

But Lamarr had another, ultimately more important role as an inventor. During World War II, both the United States and Britain had a problem: namely, bad torpedoes. The weapon's guidance systems malfunctioned on a regular basis. Lamarr read about German submarines and their deadly accurate torpedoes. She wondered about using radio frequencies to communicate with torpedoes and guide them remotely. However, she quickly envisioned an obstacle to this communication. What if German ships tried to interfere with the radio signal? Inspired by her home radio's remote control, she hypothesized that a device was needed that could allow submarines and torpedoes to talk with one another, while at the same time jumping frequencies so that Germans could not jam the transmissions.

With this problem in mind, she attended a dinner party where she met a composer named George Antheil. The two began to work together to create what Lamarr called frequency hopping. They patented the system in 1942. The US Navy had little use for it at the time, though. Years later, however, the device inspired the idea for spread-spectrum technology, first used in car telephones. Bluetooth makes use of frequency hopping in their products, as do commercial military systems such as GPS. The device is also a component of WiFi.

WOMEN IN WORLD WAR II

When the United States declared war on Japan following the attack on Pearl Harbor, men hastened to join the war effort by the hundreds of thousands. Almost 350,000 American women joined them, serving both at home and abroad. They volunteered for organizations such as the Women's Army Auxiliary Corps (WAACs), the nurses corps for the Army and Navy, and the women's reserve for the Navy, Marine Corps, and Coast Guard. As WASPs, or members of the Women's Airforce Service Pilots, women flew American military aircraft, transporting planes from factories to air bases, joining in strafing and target missions, and moving cargo from place to place. Their efforts freed up male pilots for active duty. Of the more than one thousand WASPs, thirty-eight were killed in the line of duty.

At home, five million women joined the workforce, many taking roles that men had previously filled so they could help the war effort. They filled factories and defense plants around the nation. The aviation industry consisted of a 65 percent female workforce

(continued on the next page)

(continued from the previous page)

in 1943. The "Rosie the Riveter" recruitment campaign featured a woman wearing blue coveralls with her hair in a bandanna and her fist raised as a symbol of strength. This image appeared in newspapers, movies, posters, articles, paintings, and photographs and encouraged thousands of women to join the workforce as their patriotic duty.

The famous World War II poster featuring "Rosie the Riveter" encouraged American women to support the war effort by taking factory jobs.

Furthering Medicine

Throughout the 1940s and 1950s, women inventors made huge strides in improving medicine. One of these women was Florence Seibert (1897–1991), an American scientist best known for inventing the first reliable tuberculosis (TB) test.

Florence Barbara Seibert was born in Easton, Pennsylvania, and contracted polio at age three. The virus forced her to wear leg braces and left her with a slight limp. She could not play and run like other children, so she concentrated on her education. After graduating at the top of her high school class, she earned university degrees in chemistry and zoology (1918), and during World War I she worked as a chemist in a paper mill. A scholarship to Yale University enabled her to earn a PhD in biochemistry in 1923. During her doctorate work, she discovered that patients could contract fevers if intravenous (IV) injections were made with contaminated distilled water. In order to eliminate the bacteria that was causing the sickness, she invented a distillation process, which increased the safety of IV drug therapy. It also improved the safety of blood transfusions during surgery.

While working in Sweden as a Guggenheim fellow (1937–1938), she developed a procedure for isolating protein molecules in tuberculosis. She then used these molecules to create a skin test that would determine whether or not a person had TB. TB is a bacterial infection that affects the lungs. It is

Dr. Florence Barbara Seibert announced her discovery of an important tuberculin molecule at a meeting of the National Tuberculosis Association in Los Angeles, California.

extremely infectious during an active outbreak, but it can go dormant after infection, making it difficult to detect. Seibert's test became standard in the United States in 1941 and in 1952 by the World Health Organization. It is still in use today.

Soldiers in World War II suffered from a variety of fungal infections for which there was little treatment. In 1948, Elizabeth Hazen worked at the New York State Department of Health and Rachel Brown worked for the state as a chemist out of Albany. Hazen was trying to develop an antifungal medicine. Brown supplied Hazen with specific types of bacteria to aid her research and did it by sending soil samples in mason jars and mailing them back and forth through the US Postal Service for analysis. This collaboration led to the development of nystatin, the first medication for treating fungal infections. In 1957, Brown and Hazen received a patent for nystatin. Some fungal infections are minor, such as athlete's foot, but others can be deadly, such as those that occur during organ transplants, AIDS, and chemotherapy. Nystatin has also been used for unlikely purposes, such as treating Dutch elm disease in trees and fixing water and mold damage in artwork.

A Multitude of Drugs

Gertrude Belle Elion, who was born in New York City in 1918, entered college to study chemistry at the age

Gertrude "Trudy" Belle Elion is shown here around 1988. The daughter of immigrants, she had to join the workforce before completing her PhD.

of fifteen. After earning her bachelor's degree, she became the only female in her class as she studied for her master's degree in 1939. Although she had previously encountered difficulty finding a lab job due to her gender, the coming of World War II changed everything for her. She said, "Whatever reservations there were about employing women in laboratories simply evaporated."

In 1944, she took a position at the Burroughs Wellcome Laboratories, which later became known as GlaxoSmithKline. There, she worked with George H. Hitchings, a collaboration that lasted for the next forty years. The two pioneered innovative research methods that departed from the typical trial and error approach that had been in use before this. Instead, Elion and Hitchings looked for differences between healthy human cells and those of viruses, bacteria, and cancer cells. The information they gained allowed them to create drugs that would either destroy or inhibit the unhealthy pathogen, while leaving the normal cells undamaged. These drugs treated leukemia, urinary-tract infections, gout, autoimmune disorders, viral herpes, kidney transplant rejection, and malaria.

In 1988, she shared a Nobel Prize for Physiology or Medicine with colleagues George H. Hitchings and Sir James W. Black. After her official retirement in 1983, she continued to assist with the development of the first drug used to treat AIDS, azidothymidine, or AZT.

EYE IN THE SKY

African American Marie Van Brittan Brown (1922–1999) was a nurse and inventor who invented a precursor to the modern home TV security system. The high crime in Brown's New York City neighborhood made Brown feel unsafe—so did the fact that police sometimes did not respond to emergencies. Brown and her husband invented a way for a motorized camera to peer through a set of peepholes and project images onto a TV monitor. The device also included a two-way microphone to speak with a person outside and an emergency alarm button to notify the police. The patent for the Browns' closed circuit television security system was approved on December 2, 1969.

Women in Industry

Allene Rosalinde Jeanes (1906–1995) discovered one of the most widely used food substances in the world, the thickening and texturizing agent known as xanthan gum in the 1950s.

Jeanes, born in Waco, Texas, earned her bachelor's degree from Baylor College, then went on to the University of California at Berkeley to obtain her master's degree. In 1938, she earned a PhD in organic chemistry from the University of Illinois. She spent her career working for the US government, first for the National Institutes of Health in Washington, D.C., and later for the US Department of Agriculture's Northern Regional Research Lab (NRRL). There, she studied polymers, large molecules found in corn, wheat, and wood. One of her discoveries came when a soft-drink company sent her a bad batch of root beer and asked her to find out what had happened to it. In the course of her investigation, she discovered that it was contaminated with a kind of bacteria that produced dextran, a microbe first discovered by Louis Pasteur in wine. Prior to Jeanes's discovery, dextran could not be mass-produced.

In 1950, when the United States entered the Korean War, dextran was used in order to extend blood plasma, keeping a person who had lost a large volume of blood alive long enough to receive a transfusion. Dextran's use in the war saved many lives and began to be used in the civilian world as well in 1953.

After this discovery, Jeanes invented a process for making xanthan gum, a substance created by the bacteria *Xanthomonas campestris* as it ferments. Xanthan gum is used in foods, medicines, cosmetics, and in the gas and oil industry to extract fossil fuels from the earth.

Over her career, Jeanes received ten patents and produced dozens of publications. In 1953, she became the first woman to receive the Distinguished Service Award from the US Department of Agriculture and later received other honors from the American

Chemical Society and the US Civil Service Commission.

Computing Power

Grace Murray Hopper (1906–1992) is one of the most important figures in the computer age. Born in New York City, she obtained a master's degree and PhD in mathematics from Yale University. She taught mathematics at Vassar College until the outbreak of World War II. She then joined the US Navy's Women's Reserves in 1943 and was assigned to work on the Mark I, one of the world's first computers. She needed to program the machine—it was fifty-one feet (sixteen meters) long and eight feet (two meters) high—to calculate missile trajectories. While there, she coined the term "bug" to refer to computer failures after a moth became stuck in the circuits.

Grace Murray Hopper was an inventor, mathematician, and rear admiral in the US Navy. In 1969, she was named the "Man of the Year" by the Data Processing Management Association.

Hopper's computer experience helped her when she went to work in private industry following the war. There, she created the first computer compiler in order to translate libraries of program code into binary code capable of being read by a computer. In 1957, she remained at her place of employment—now Sperry Rand Corporation—when her division developed the first data-processing compiler in English. It was called Flow-Matic and served as one of the main models during the development of the computing language COBOL. After its introduction in 1960, COBOL became the most widely used computer language and is still used in large-scale programming.

CHAPTER SEVEN

WOMEN MAKE WAVES: THE LATE TWENTIETH CENTURY

W omen in the late twentieth century experienced a multitude of benefits from the women's rights movement in the 1960s and 1970s. Feminists support equality with men in different spheres of influence, including social, economic, and political. This movement resulted in more women taking a greater role in the workforce, government, and in arguing for social issues like abortion rights, child care, and better wages. Sexism began to be brought to light as well as violence against women, both in the home and out of it.

It was in this environment that, while working for a computing giant in the 1960s, computer scientist Lynn Conway invented dynamic instruction scheduling, a revolutionary way of improving the computer chip's processing power. But when she began her gender transition in 1967, she was fired and her achievements were forgotten for decades. Despite this setback, Conway authored an influential textbook on very-large-scale-integration (VLSI) technology and taught the first course at the Massachusetts Institute of Technology (MIT) on the subject. The military's Defense Advanced Research Projects Agency (DARPA) recruited her, unaware of her past accomplishments. She began coming out as transgender in the late 1990s, and the full body of her life's work has finally been recognized.

Potent Polymers

Stephanie Kwolek (1923–2014) was a chemist born in New Kensington, Pennsylvania. Her mother raised her and her brother alone after her father died when she was ten years old. She received a degree in chemistry from Carnegie Institute of Technology in 1946 with the intention of going to medical school. But a lack of funds caused her to take a job as a lab chemist for DuPont, where she remained for her entire career. The company had created nylon just before World War II, and it pursued the new field of synthetic fibers. Along with a team of chemists, Kwolek began to investigate new polymer fibers. During the 1950s and 1960s, Kwolek worked with one polymer in particular—aromatic polyamides—

which could be fashioned into stiff, strong, flame-resistant fibers. This work resulted in a compound called Nomex, released in 1961 as a flame-resistant fiber. Her work in liquid crystal polymers resulted in the creation of a fiber material stronger than any which had been previously developed. In 1971, this material, known as Kevlar, entered the marketplace and was used in tire cords, boat hulls, and lightweight bulletproof vests, among other things.

Describing her forty-year career, she said, "I'm very conscientious. And I discovered over the years that I seem to see things that other people did not see. If things don't work out I don't just throw them out. I struggle over them, to try and see if there's something there."

In 1952, research chemist Patsy Sherman was working in the lab at the 3M Company, one of only a few women in the field. One of her assistants accidentally dropped a container filled with a liquid rubber substance on the floor. Some of it splashed onto Sherman's canvas shoes, where it dried but was impossible to wash off. It didn't budge with either water and solvents, which made both substances run off "like water off a duck's back."

Sherman and colleague Sam Smith worked for three years to improve the chemicals and make them less costly to produce. In 1971, Sherman finished the mixture and patented it. It became a well-known product: Scotchgard.

Sherman gave these words of encouragement to potential inventors: "Anyone can become an inventor, as long as they keep an open and inquiring mind and never overlook the possible significance of an accident or apparent failure."

WOMEN'S MEDICINE

For many years, drug research was conducted only on men or male laboratory animals. The research was then applied to both genders as if there were no differences in how drugs affected them. However, women do respond to medications differently. In fact, women are more likely to have adverse effects from medicine—50 to 75 percent more likely. Women's biology affects how certain illnesses present. Heart attacks are one example. Women may have pain in the jaw or shoulder or no symptoms whatsoever. Half of women have no pain in the chest during a heart attack. Instead, women may have indigestion, shortness of breath, unusual fatigue, or even flulike symptoms. The longer a woman waits to obtain treatment, the less chance she has to survive. Certain risk factors are greater for women, too. Smoking increases a woman's chance of having a heart attack sevenfold. Diabetes and depression are also significant risk factors.

Lung cancer, Alzheimer's disease, and cardiovascular disease also present differently in women than men. Because of this, women are often misdiagnosed.

Women had been routinely excluded from drug trials funded by the National Institutes of Health until a federal law prohibited this in 1993. While the number of women included in medication studies has increased over the subsequent years, there is still a significant gender gap.

Seeing Straight

Dr. Patricia Bath (1942–) revolutionized the field of ophthalmology with the invention of the Laserphaco Probe, a device that used lasers to perform cataract surgery. She patented the invention in 1988, becoming the first African American woman doctor to receive a medical patent.

Bath was born in Harlem, New York, where she excelled in her studies, winning scientific research awards starting at age sixteen. She earned her medical degree and went on to become the first African American resident in ophthalmology while at New York University. While she worked as an intern in Harlem, she noticed that half of her patients suffered from visual impairment or blindness. However, when she worked at Columbia University, she encountered few blind patients. She completed a study, which revealed that blacks were twice as likely as whites to experience blindness. She founded a discipline called community ophthalmology, in which volunteer eye workers offer care and treatment

Dr. Patricia Bath is shown here as she attends the Tribeca Disruptive Innovation Awards held during the Tribeca Film Festival in 2012.

to underserved populations in senior centers and senior care programs.

Bath moved to the University of California, Los Angeles (UCLA) in 1974, where she became an assistant professor of surgery and ophthalmology, becoming the first woman faculty member at UCLA's Jules Stein Eye Institute. The office she was offered was located "in the basement next to the lab animals." She refused it until she obtained a better office location. While still at UCLA in 1983, she became the first woman to chair an ophthalmology residency program in the United States. She also cofounded the American Institute for the Prevention of Blindness.

In 1981, she began to work on what became the Laserphaco probe to remove cataracts. It took her five years, but the device is now in use across the world. A high point for her was using her device to restore the sight of several people who had been blind for over thirty years.

She said, "my love of humanity and passion for helping others inspired me to become a physician." This love helped her overcome the obstacles of poverty, sexism, and racism she experienced as a pioneer in her field.

Medical Mysteries Solved

Rosalyn Yalow (1921–2011) was a medical physicist who shared a 1977 Nobel Prize in Medicine with

Dr. Rosalyn Yalow, shown here in her lab in October 1977, researched hormones at the Bronx Veterans Administration Hospital for thirty years.

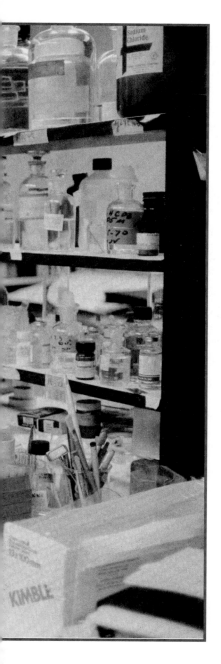

Andrew V. Schally and Roger Guillemin for the development of the radioimmunoassay (RIA) technique.

Born in New York City, she entered the graduate program at the University of Illinois where she studied nuclear physics. Once, after receiving an A- in an optics lab course, the department chairman declared, "that A- confirms that women do not do well at laboratory work." Regardless, she earned her doctorate in 1945.

She taught physics for several years before consulting for the Bronx Veterans Administration Medical Center, where she built the nuclear research program from the ground up. Afterward, she began to work with radioactive isotopes.

In the 1950s, diabetes was thought to develop because of a lack of insulin. At the time, it was impossible to measure substances as small as insulin. Yalow and Dr. Solomon Berson created a technique for measuring levels of insulin known as radioimmunoassay (RIA) and proved that type 2 diabetes results from the body's inefficient use of insulin. The discovery led to better treatment for diabetes, mental retardation, and other conditions. In the years since the invention of RIA, it has become a basic testing and research method adopted by nearly all medical labs worldwide.

Another influential medical inventor is Mary-Claire King (1946–). A geneticist, her doctoral work demonstrated that humans and chimpanzees share 99 percent of the same genes, a finding that made news worldwide. After years of lab work tracking hundreds of data points, she also identified the genetic markers of breast cancer. The discovery of this gene, BRCA1, transformed both diagnosis and treatment for breast cancer. Outside of work, she used her talents to create genetic tests to help identify victims of political assassinations in Argentina and other countries.

CHAPTER EIGHT

HOW FAR WILL WOMEN GO? THE TWENTY-FIRST CENTURY AND BEYOND

Women's achievements in science, medicine, industry, and the arts continue to grow by leaps and bounds as the new millennium has dawned. While plenty of room remains for inventions of less-than-global scope, women who are increasingly entering the ranks of science, technology, engineering, and mathematics (STEM) are creating significant change for society.

One such woman is chemical biologist Carolyn Bertozzi (1966–). As a Stanford University professor, she studies how cells communicate with each other through sugars. She invented the world's first bioorthogonal (her term) chemical reactions that occur inside living systems and do not interfere with natural biochemical processes. These reactions can be used for labeling specific molecules in cells and for imaging or monitoring molecular changes in disease progression. Bertozzi's work has furthered research in cancer, inflammation, and bacterial infections. In 1999, she became a MacArthur Fellow, and in 2010 Bertozzi was the first woman to win the $500,000 Lemelson-MIT prize.

Women and Technology

Dr. Shirley Jackson (1946–) has a prominent listing in the National Women's Hall of Fame—and for good reason. She is the first African American woman to receive a doctorate from MIT, and one of two African American women to receive a doctorate in physics. As a theoretical physicist who worked at the former AT&T Bell Laboratories, she has been credited with many advances in technology, which led to the invention of the portable fax, touch-tone telephone, solar cells, fiber-optic cables, and the technology enabling caller ID and call waiting. She is the first black woman to be named chair of the US Nuclear Regulatory Commission and in 2016 was given the National Medal of Science, the nation's highest honor for scientific achievement by President Barack Obama.

Angela Belcher (1968–) is an inventor and biological engineer, who is one of the leading experts in nanotechnology. She genetically

Dr. Shirley Jackson receives the National Medal of Science from President Barack Obama in 2016. The medal recognizes people who have made important contributions in science and engineering.

engineers viruses to create new products, work that has resulted in "self-assembled" materials that may be used as components in electronic devices such as batteries, display screens, and fuel cells. She has won numerous awards and honors, authored more than twenty papers, and holds some twenty patents or patents pending. She is a professor of materials science and engineering and bioengineering at MIT.

SMARTPHONES AND CLEAN WATER

Gitanjali Rao, as an eleven-year-old seventh grader, hopes to become a geneticist or epidemiologist in the future. She has already made strides toward that goal by winning the 2017 Discovery Education 3M Young Scientist Challenge for her invention of a lead-detection device. She got the idea when she saw her parents testing the water in their Colorado home following revelations about contaminated water in Flint, Michigan. She noticed that the water-testing options were slow and undependable. She told Business Insider, "Well, this is not a reliable process and I've got to do something to change this."

She found information on MIT's Material Science and Engineering website about new technology to identify hazardous materials. Then, she approached local high schools and universities to use their labs to experiment and create a three-part device that contains a disposable carbon cartridge, an Arduino signal processor with Bluetooth, and a smartphone app that displays the results. When the cartridge is immersed in water, information is sent to the smartphone that alerts the owner whether the water is contaminated with lead or not.

Gitanjali Rao displays her "Tethys" device in November 2017 at the STEM School Highlands Ranch in Colorado.

New Solutions to Old Problems

Taiwan-born Anne Chiang (1942–) came to the University of Southern California (USC) to earn a doctorate in physical chemistry in 1968. As a scientist for Memorex Corporation, she invented microfilm for computer data recording. In 1971, she began working with Xerox to invent display devices and a phototransistor. She is best known for her work in thin-film transistor technology, or TFT, in the 1980s and 1990s. This work enabled the creation of lightweight, portable flat panel display personal computers. It also created innovations in medical radiography by improving the resolution of images, which helps doctors more accurately diagnose patients.

Canadian Eva Vertes, born in Toronto, Canada, in 1986, started her scientific career young. By age fifteen, she had uncovered properties of a chemical compound called RPI-069 that stopped fruit flies' brain cells from dying. At age seventeen, she exhibited her findings at the International Science Fair and won the Best in Medicine award. Her research could lead to a groundbreaking new treatment for patients afflicted with Alzheimer's disease. She then moved on to earn an MD from the University of Florida and to research involving stem cells and cancer.

Turkish scientist Canan Dagdeviren (1985–) created a skin sensor that can help diagnose skin cancer. In skin cancer, an early sign is that an area of skin is slightly thicker than the surrounding tissue.

ANIMALS AND AUTISM

Temple Grandin (1947–) is unusual in the annals of invention. By the time she turned three, she could not talk and also demonstrated numerous behavioral problems. A diagnosis of autism followed. Her parents were counseled to place her in an institution, but instead they sent her to private schools, where she could cultivate her high IQ. She earned a bachelor's degree afterward, followed by a master's degree in animal science from Arizona State University and then a PhD in animal science from the University of Illinois at Urbana-Champaign.

She realized that she shared with animals heightened fear due to increased sensitivity to sound and touch. She designed a "squeeze machine" for her own use while still in high school. It was modeled

(continued on the next page)

Temple Grandin has authored a number of books about living with autism and understanding the social behavior of both animals and humans.

(continued from the previous page)

on a livestock chute used to administer vaccinations and perform other procedures. This machine helped to release her anxiety. Advanced designs of this invention are widely used in autism treatment. Her life's work, however, has been in designing livestock facilities in order to lessen the pain and fear during the slaughtering of livestock.

Dagdeviren's sensor measures the variations in skin density more accurately than doctors can do by touch. As a PhD student at the University of Illinois, she also developed a device that is permanently implanted inside the body. The device draws its energy from the organs' movements and sends it to pacemakers and similar devices to power them. This could make life easier for pacemaker recipients, whose bulky batteries must be surgically replaced every five to eight years. Dagdeviren's achievements were recognized in 2015 when she was named one of the "Top 35 Innovators Under 35" by *MIT Technology Review*.

What does the future hold for other women inventors? Perhaps more successes like those of Lisa Seacat DeLuca, who is the most prolific female inventor in IBM's history, having filed more than 370 patent applications. Her inventions make use of the latest technology and social media applications.

She uses the crowdfunding website Kickstarter to fund some projects, apps like If This Then That (IFTTT), and technology such as 3D printers. Some of her inventions include a guidance system for smartphone users that keeps them from losing power as they walk; a necklace that lights up when it detects the use of a certain Twitter hashtag; an alert for people on conference calls when a certain person or topic comes up; and a locator that tracks lost items in cars.

DeLuca told *MIT Technology Review*, "The idea generation isn't the slow part. Anyone can come up with ideas very quickly. It's taking the time to write them down and do research to figure out if it's a great idea or how to make it an even better idea—that's really the bottleneck in innovation."

New women inventors are making discoveries at an accelerating pace at the beginning of the millennium. Who knows what will come next?

TIMELINE

30,000 BCE Mortar and pestle first used.

13,000 BCE Pottery begins to be used.

5,000 BCE The loom is invented.

100 BCE Maria the Jewess invents the double boiler.

ca. 1280 Granny Huang invents the cotton gin in China.

1712 Sybilla Masters received a patent for her corn cleaning and curing device; she becomes the first American female inventor.

1793 Hannah Slater invents better cotton thread.

1811 Sarah Guppy Coote patents bridge supports in England.

1843 Ada Lovelace devises the concept of looping, critical for the later development of computers.

1871 Margaret E. Knight patents a paper bag machine for mass production.

1886 Josephine G. Cochran invents the first practical dishwasher.

1903 Mary Anderson patents windshield wipers.
Marie Curie receives the Nobel Prize for her work in radioactivity.

1905 Madame C. J. Walker devises hair treatments for black women.

1923 Ma Rainey begins recording blues for Paramount.

1937–38 Florence Seibert develops the first reliable TB (tuberculosis) test.

1942 Hedy Lamarr patents the frequency-hopping system.

1957 Grace Murray Hopper's data-processing compiler in English leads to the development of the computing language COBOL.

1971 Stephanie Kwolek's invention of Kevlar hits the market.

1977 Rosalyn Yalow receives the Nobel Prize for her development of the radioimmunoassay (RIA) technique.

1988 Gertrude Elion receives the Nobel Prize for her work developing drugs to treat a range of health conditions.
Patricia Bath uses lasers to perform cataract surgery.

1980s–90s Anne Chiang creates thin-film transistor technology.

1990 Mary-Claire King discovers the breast cancer gene BRCA1.

2003 Carolyn Bertozzi develops bioorthogonal chemical reactions.

GLOSSARY

analytical engine A proposed mechanical general-purpose computer.

annotating Adding notes or comments to.

apparatus A tool or piece of equipment for a specific purpose.

autism A disorder that appears in children prior to age three and affects an individual's ability to communicate and form normal relationships. The disoder may also involve repetitive actions for some individuals.

binary code A system that uses the digits 0 and 1 to represent a letter, digit, or other character in a computer.

caulking Making something tight against leakage.

disparities Distinctions in character or quality.

distill To transform a liquid by the use of evaporation and condensation.

hypothesized Made or suggested.

intravenous Entering a vein.

invalid An ill person.

isolate To separate from another substance in order to create a pure result.

medium A person who claims to communicate with the dead.

ophthalmology A type of medicine that deals with diseases of the eye.

pathogen An agent that causes a disease.

physiology A type of biology dealing with the function of living organs, tissues, or cells.

precursor A cell or substance from which another cell or substance is formed.

prototype An example or model.

shuttle In weaving, a device that passes the thread of the weft between the threads of the warp.

spiritualism A belief that spirits of the dead contact the living by the use of a medium.

still A device used in the distillation process.

suspension bridge A bridge that is suspended on cables between towers.

FOR MORE INFORMATION

Canadian Multicultural Inventors Museum
(416) 839-2442
Website: http://multiculturalmuseums.org
Facebook: @multiculturalinventors
A nonprofit traveling museum whose goal is "to
   create awareness of inventors from all parts of
   the globe, all races, all religions, all genders, all
   sexual orientations and all disabilities."

National Inventors Hall of Fame and Museum
USPTO, Madison Building
600 Dulany Street
Alexandria, VA 22314
(571) 272-0095
Website: http://www.invent.org/honor/hall-of-fame
   -museum
Facebook and Twitter: @InventorsHOF
Instagram: @inventionproject
The site's mission is "to recognize inventors and
   invention, celebrate our country's rich, innovative
   history, inspire creativity, and advance the spirit of
   innovation and entrepreneurship."

Smithsonian Institution
Jerome and Dorothy Lemelson Center for the Study of
   Invention and Innovation
National Museum of American History

Room 1210, MRC 604
14th Street and Constitution Avenue NW
Mailing address:
PO Box 37012
Washington, DC 20013-7012
(202) 633-3656
Website: http://invention.si.edu
Facebook: @lemelsoncenter
Twitter: @SI_Invention
Instagram: @si_invention
The mission of the Lemelson Center is to "document,
    interpret, and disseminate information about
    invention and innovation; encourage inventive
    creativity in young people; and foster an
    appreciation for the central role of invention and
    innovation in the history of the United States."

Toronto International Society of Innovation &
    Advanced Skills (TISIAS)
#2508 - 18 Spring Garden Avenue
North York, ON M2N 7M2
Canada
(647) 554-3998
Website: http://www.tisias.org
Facebook: @inventorsound
TISIAS supports students, inventors, innovators,
    entrepreneurs, and researchers across Canada,
    the United States, and Korea in order to
    encourage creative ideas and innovative projects.

United Inventors Association of America
1025 Connecticut Avenue, Suite 1000

Washington DC 20036
Website: http://www.uiausa.org
Facebook and Twitter: @uiausa
This nonprofit educational organization provides
    resources to the inventing community and
    encourages ethics in the industry. It organizes
    clubs and events, as well as providing resources
    and information designed to help support the
    community of independent inventors.

United States Patent and Trademark Office
USPTO Kids
(800) 786-9199
Website: https://www.uspto.gov/kids
Facebook: @uspto.gov
Twitter: @uspto
Designed to demystify the patent and trademark
    process, this site has videos, activities, links,
    downloads, and more for teen inventors.

Women Inventors and Innovators
(707) 486-2441
Website: http://www.womeninventorsandinnovators
    .org/home.html
This mural project is designed to delve into
    women's accomplishments and value the
    contributions of the past and present. The
    project's ultimate goal is to close the wage gap
    between women and men.

FOR FURTHER READING

Braun, Sandra. *Women Inventors Who Changed the World*. New York, NY: Rosen Publishing, 2012.

Challone, Jack. *Exploring the Mysteries of Genius and Invention*. New York, NY: Rosen Publishing, 2017.

De la Rosa, Jeff. *Meet NASA Inventor Kendra Short and Her Printable Probes and Cosmic Confetti*. Chicago, IL: World Book, Inc., 2017.

Felix, Rebecca. *Temple Grandin*. Minneapolis, MN: Super Sandcastle, 2017.

Hepplewhite, Peter, and Mairi Campbell. *All About ... The Industrial Revolution*. London, England: Wayland, 2015.

Labrecque, Ellen. *Patricia Bath and Laser Surgery*. Ann Arbor, MI: Cherry Lake Publishing, 2017.

May, Vicki V., and Allison Bruce. *Engineering: Cool Women Who Design*. White River Junction, VT: Nomad Press, 2016.

Noyce, Pendred. *Magnificent Minds: Sixteen Pioneering Women in Science and Medicine*. Boston, MA: Tumblehome Learning, Inc., 2016.

Stanley, Diane, and Jessie Hartland. *Ada Lovelace, Poet of Science: The First Computer Programmer*. New York, NY: Simon & Schuster Books for Young Readers, 2016.

Swaby, Rachel. *Trailblazers: 33 Women in Science Who Changed the World*. New York, NY: Delacorte Press, 2016.

BIBLIOGRAPHY

Abrams, Michael. "Margaret Knight." ASME, June 2012. https://www.asme.org/engineering-topics/articles/diversity/margaret-knight.

Arizona State University, Institute of Human Origins. "Lucy's Story." Retrieved September 6, 2017. https://iho.asu.edu/about/lucys-story.

Bedi, Joyce. *Exploring the History of Women Inventors. Smithsonian National Museum of American History.* Retrieved September 6, 2017. http://invention.si.edu/exploring-history-women-inventors.

Brown, David E. *Inventing Modern America: From the Microwave to the Mouse.* Cambridge, MA: The MIT Press, 2002.

Celebrating America's Women Physicians. "Dr. Louise Pearce." USA.gov, June 3, 2015. https://cfmedicine.nlm.nih.gov/physicians/biography_248.html.

Centers for Disease Control and Prevention. "History of Smallpox." August 30, 2016. https://www.cdc.gov/smallpox/history/history.html.

Changing the Face of Medicine, U.S. National Library of Medicine, National Institutes of Health. "Dr. Patricia E. Bath." June 3, 2015. https://cfmedicine.nlm.nih.gov/physicians/biography_26.html.

Chemical Heritage Foundation. "Elizabeth Lee Hazen and Rachel Fuller Brown." Retrieved on September 6, 2017. https://www.chemheritage.org/historical-profile/elizabeth-lee-hazen-and-rachel-fuller-brown.

"Diaper, US Patent 355368A." January 4, 1887.
https://www.google.com/patents/US355368.

Dreifus, Claudia. "A Never-Ending Genetic Quest."
New York Times, February 9, 2015. https://www
.nytimes.com/2015/02/10/science/mary-claire
-kings-pioneering-gene-work-from-breast-cancer-to
-human-rights.html.

Giges, Nancy. "Lillian Moller Gilbreth." ASME, May
2012. https://www.asme.org/career-education
/articles/management-professional-practice
/lillian-moller-gilbreth.

Gould, Suzanne. "AAUW Member Saves Lives: Dr.
Louise Pearce." AAUW, August 17, 2015. http://
www.aauw.org/2015/08/17/louise-pearce.

Herran, Kathy Neill. "Harriet Morrison Irwin: The
House That Harriet Built." NCPedia, Reprinted with
permission from the Tar Heel Junior Historian, Fall
2006. Tar Heel Junior Historian Association, NC
Museum of History. https://www.ncpedia.org
/biography/irwin-harriet-morrison.

Inventricity.com. "Charlotte Smith: Inventors
Champion." Retrieved September 6, 2017. http://
www.inventricity.com/charlotte-smith-inventors
-champion.

Jacobs, Suzanne. "Deluca, Lisa Seacat." *MIT
Technology Review*. Retrieved September 6, 2017.
https://www.technologyreview.com/lists
/innovators-under-35/2015/inventor/lisa-seacat
-deluca.

Lambert, Bruce. "Dr. Florence B. Seibert, Inventor Of
Standard TB Test, Dies at 93." *New York Times*,
August 31, 1991. http://www.nytimes

.com/1991/08/31/us/dr-florence-b-seibert -inventor-of-standard-tb-test-dies-at-93.html.

Leinhard, John H. "No. 326: Colonial Women Inventors." Engines of Our Ingenuity. http://www .uh.edu/engines/epi326.htm.

Lemelson-MIT. "Gertrude Belle Elion." Retrieved September 6, 2017. http://lemelson.mit.edu /resources/gertrude-belle-elion.

"Letters Patent No. 94,116." United States Patent Office. August 24, 1869. http://pdfpiw.uspto.gov

Maggs, Sam. *Wonder Women: 25 Innovators, Inventors, and Trailblazers Who Changed History*. Philadelphia, PA: Quirk Books, 2016.

Mehta, Laxmi. "Heart Attacks Are Different in Women—and It's Time We Treat Them That Way." *US News & World Report*, March 14, 2016. https:// health.usnews.com/health-news/patient-advice /articles/2016-03-14/heart-attacks-are-different-in -women-and-its-time-we-treat-them-that-way.

National WWII Museum. "American Women in World War II: On the Home Front and Beyond." Retrieved September 6, 2017. https://www .nationalww2museum.org/students-teachers /student-resources/research-starters/women -wwii.

O'Brien, Dennis. "A Root Beer-Based Discovery that Saved Lives." USDA, November 9, 2016. https:// www.usda.gov/media/blog/2016/11/9/root-beer -based-discovery-saved-lives.

Patai, Raphael. *The Jewish Alchemists*. Princeton, NJ: Princeton University Press, 1994.

Skylar, Julia. "Canan Dagdeviren, 30." *MIT Technology Review*. Retrieved September 6, 2017. https://www.technologyreview.com/lists/innovators-under-35/2015/inventor/canan-dagdeviren.

Smith, Charlotte, ed. *The Woman Inventor*. Patent Centennial Celebration. Washington, DC: 1891. https://archive.org/details/Womaninventor1Smit.

Sobel, Dava. *The Glass Universe: How the Ladies of the Harvard Observatory Took the Measure of the Stars*. New York, NY: Viking, 2016.

United States Patent and Trademark Office. "Woman Invented Dishwasher." December 27, 2001. https://www.uspto.gov/about-us/news-updates/woman-invented-dishwasher.

Wamsley, Laurel. "Troubled By Flint Water Crisis, 11-Year-Old Girl Invents Lead-Detecting Device." NPR, October 20, 2017. http://www.npr.org/sections/thetwo-way/2017/10/20/559071028/troubled-by-flint-water-crisis-11-year-old-girl-invents-lead-detecting-device.

INDEX

About the Author

Xina M. Uhl has written numerous educational books for young people, in addition to textbooks, teacher's guides, lessons, assessment questions, and more. She has tackled subjects including women, history, biographies, technology, and health concerns. The sole invention she lays claim to is sunglasses that block peripheral vision. These sunglasses keep motion sickness from bothering her as she reads in the car, but the product has so far remained lost in obscurity. Her blog details her publications as well as interesting facts and the occasional cat picture.

Photo Credits

Cover Hulton Archive/Getty Images; pp. 7, 48, 68, 84–85 Bettmann /Getty Images; pp. 12–13 DEA/G. Dagli Orti/De Agostini /Getty Images; p. 14 Agostini Picture Library/Getty Images; p. 17 Philippe Wojazer/AFP/Getty Images; p. 21 Lebrecht Music and Arts Photo Library/Alamy Stock Photo; p. 26 Pictorial Press Ltd /Alamy Stock Photo; pp. 28, 66 Historical/Corbis Historical /Getty Images; pp. 32–33 Epics/Hulton Archive/Getty Images; p. 35 Print Collector/Hulton Archive/Getty Images; pp. 38–39 Fine Art Photographic/Corbis Historical/Getty Images; pp. 43, 51 National Archives; p. 46 Chicago History Museum/Archive Photos /Getty Images; p. 53 Michael Ochs Archives/Getty Images; p. 54 Robert Abbott Sengstacke/Archive Photos/Getty Images; p. 57 JP Jazz Archive/Redferns/Getty Images; p. 59 Everett Historical /Shutterstock.com; p. 63 Sunset Boulevard/Corbis Historical /Getty Images; p. 70 Derek Hudson/Hulton Archive/Getty Images; pp. 74–75 Cynthia Johnson/The LIFE Images Collection /Getty Images; p. 82 Jemal Countess/Getty Images; p. 89 Drew Angerer/Getty Images; p. 91 Kathryn Scott/Denver Post /Getty Images; p. 93 Kathy Hutchins/Shutterstock.com; cover and interior pages (gold) R-studio/Shutterstock.com.

Design and Layout: Nicole Russo-Duca; Editor and Photo Researcher: Heather Moore Niver